Cambridge Plain Texts

FULLER

THE HOLY STATE
(II. 1–15)

T0346140

FULLER

THE HOLY STATE

(II. 1–15)

CAMBRIDGE

AT THE UNIVERSITY PRESS

1921

CAMBRIDGE UNIVERSITY PRESS
Cambridge, New York, Melbourne, Madrid, Cape Town,
Singapore, São Paulo, Delhi, Mexico City

Cambridge University Press
The Edinburgh Building, Cambridge CB2 8RU, UK

Published in the United States of America by Cambridge University Press, New York

www.cambridge.org
Information on this title: www.cambridge.org/9781107697362

© Cambridge University Press 1921

This publication is in copyright. Subject to statutory exception
and to the provisions of relevant collective licensing agreements,
no reproduction of any part may take place without the written
permission of Cambridge University Press.

First published 1921
Re-issued 2013

A catalogue record for this publication is available from the British Library

ISBN 978-1-107-69736-2 Paperback

Cambridge University Press has no responsibility for the persistence or
accuracy of URLs for external or third-party internet websites referred to in
this publication, and does not guarantee that any content on such websites is,
or will remain, accurate or appropriate.

NOTE

The Holy State of THOMAS FULLER (1608–1661) was printed at Cambridge by Roger Daniel, University printer, in 1642.

Educated at Cambridge, of which university he was one of the earliest historians, Fuller was a stout royalist and served for a time as a chaplain in the King's army. Had he lived longer, the Restoration would no doubt have brought him a bishopric.

In *The Holy State* the seventeenth century 'character' is treated in a style which exhibits the peculiar genius of the writer; biographical illustrations are frequently added and the general reflections of the moralist are supplemented by humorous anecdotes drawn from wide reading and from personal experience.

Fuller's temperament was that of the antiquary who must have his joke. He wrote several histories (*The Historie of the Holy Warre*, *The Church-History of Britain*, *The History of the Worthies of England*) and, though his interest in history, in ethics, in theology was the genuine interest of a scholar, he often reminds us of that would-be philosopher, Mr Edwards, upon whom cheerfulness was always breaking in.

"God bless thee, dear old man!" wrote Coleridge, "May I meet with thee!—which is tantamount to—may I go to Heaven!"

S. C. ROBERTS

December 1920

CONTENTS

THE HOLY STATE

THE SECOND BOOK

CHAP. I

The good Advocate

HE is one that will not plead that cause, wherein his tongue must be confuted by his conscience. It is the praise of the Spanish souldier, that (whilest all other Nations are mercenary, and for money will serve on any side) he will never fight against his own King: nor will our Advocate against the Sovereigne Truth, plainly appearing to his conscience.

He not onely hears but examines his Client, and pincheth the cause, where he fears it is foundred. For many Clients in telling their case rather plead then relate it, so that the Advocate hears not the true state of it, till opened by the adverse party. Surely the Lawyer that fills himself with instructions will travell longest in the cause without tiring. Others that are so quick in searching, seldome search to the quick; and those miraculous apprehensions who understand more then all, before the Client hath told half, runne without their errand, and will return without their answer.

If the matter be doubtfull, he will onely warrant his own diligence. Yet some keep an Assurance-office in their chamber, and will warrant any cause brought unto them, as knowing that if they fail they lose nothing but what long since was lost, their credit.

He makes not a Trojan-siege of a suit, but seeks to bring it to a set battel in a speedy triall. Yet sometimes suits are continued by their difficulty, the potencie and stomach of the parties, without any default in the Lawyer. Thus have there depended suits in Glocestershire, betwixt the Heirs of the Lord Barkley, and Sʳ. Thomas Talbot Viscount Lisle, ever since the reigne of King Edward the fourth untill now lately they were finally compounded.

He is faithfull to the side that first retains him. Not like Demosthenes, who secretly wrote one oration for Phormio, and another in the same matter for Apolidorus his adversary.

In pleading he shoots fairly at the head of the cause, and having fastened, no frowns nor favours shall make him let go his hold. Not snatching aside here and there, to no purpose, speaking little in much, as it was said of Anaximenes, *That he had a flood of words, and a drop of reason.* His boldnesse riseth or falleth as he apprehends the goodnesse or badnesse of his cause.

He joyes not to be retain'd in such a suit, where all the right in question, is but a drop blown up with malice to be a bubble. Wherefore in such triviall matters he perswades his Client to sound a retreat, and make a composition.

When his name is up, his industry is not down, thinking to plead not by his study but his credit. Commonly Physicians like beer are best when they are old, & Lawyers like bread when they are young and new. But our Advocate grows not lazie. And if a leading

case be out of the road of his practice, he will take
pains to trace it thorow his books, and prick the foot-
steps thereof wheresoever he finds it.

*He is more carefull to deserve, then greedy to take
fees.* He accounts the very pleading of a poore widows
honest cause sufficient fees, as conceiving himself then
the King of Heavens Advocate, bound *ex officio* to
prosecute it. And although some may say that such
a Lawyer may even go live in Cornwall, where it is
observed that few of that profession hitherto have
grown to any great livelihood, yet shall he (besides
those two felicities of common Lawyers, that they
seldome die either without heirs or making a will)
find Gods blessing on his provisions and posterity.

We will respit him a while till he comes to be a
Judge, and then we will give an example of both
together.

Chap. 2

The good Physician

*He trusteth not the single witnesse of the water if better
testimony may be had.* For reasons drawn from the
urine alone are as brittle as the urinall. Sometimes
the water runneth in such post-hast through the sick
mans body, it can give no account of any thing
memorable in the passage, though the most judicious
eye examine it. Yea the sick man may be in the state
of death, and yet life appear in his state.

*Coming to his patient he perswades him to put his
trust in God the fountain of health.* The neglect hereof
hath caused the bad success of the best Physicians:

for God will manifest that though skill comes mediately from him to be gotten by mans pains, successe comes from him immediately to be disposed at his pleasure.

He hansells not his new experiments on the bodies of his patients; letting loose mad receipts into the sick mans body, to try how well Nature in him will fight against them, whilest himself stands by and sees the battel, except it be in desperate cases when death must be expell'd by death.

To poore people he prescribes cheap but wholesome medicines: not removing the consumption out of their bodies into their purses; nor sending them to the East Indies for drugs, when they can reach better out of their gardens.

Lest his Apothecary should oversee, he oversees his Apothecary. For though many of that profession be both able and honest, yet some out of ignorance or haste may mistake: witnesse one of Bloys, who being to serve a Doctours bill, in stead of *Optimi* (short written) read *Opii*, and had sent the patient asleep to his grave, if the Doctours watchfulnesse had not prevented him; worse are those who make wilfull errours, giving one thing for another. A prodigall who had spent his estate was pleased to jeer himself, boasting that he had cosened those who had bought his means; They gave me (said he) good new money, and I sold them my Great-great-grandfathers old land. But this cosenage is too too true in many Apothecaries, selling to sick folk for new money antiquated drugs, and making dying mens Physick of dead ingredients.

He brings not news with a false spie that the coast is clear till death surprises the sick man. I know Physicians love to make the best of their patients estate. First 'tis improper that *Adjutores vitæ* should be *Nuncii mortis*. Secondly, none, with their good will, will tell bad news. Thirdly, their fee may be the worse for't. Fourthly, 'tis a confessing that their art is conquer'd. Fifthly, it will poyson their patients heart with grief, and make it break before the time. However they may so order it, that the party may be inform'd of his dangerous condition, that he be not outed of this world before he be provided for another.

When he can keep life no longer in, he makes a fair & easie passage for it to go out. He giveth his attendance for the facilitating and asswaging of the pains and agonies of death. Yet generally 'tis death to a Physician to be with a dying man.

Vnworthy pretenders to Physick are rather foils then stains to the Profession. Such a one was that counterfeit, who called himself *The Baron of Blackamore*, and feigned he was sent from the Emperour to our young King Henry the sixth, to be his principall Physician: but his forgery being discovered, he was apprehended, and executed in the Tower of London, *Anno* 1426. and such the world daily swarms with. Well did the Poets feigne Æsculapius and Circe, brother and sister, and both children of the Sunne: for in all times in the opinion of the multitude, witches, old women, and impostours have had a competition with Physicians. And commonly the most ignorant are the most confident in their undertakings, and will not stick to tell you what disease the gall of a dove is good to cure. He took himself to be no mean Doctour, who being guilty of no Greek, and being demanded why it was called an *Hectick fever*; *because* (saith he) *of an hecking cough which ever attendeth that disease.* And here it will not be amisse to describe the life of the famous Quack-salver Paracelsus, both because it is not ordinarily to be met with, and that men may see what a monster many make a miracle of learning, and propound him their pattern in their practice.

CHAP. 3

The life of PARACELSUS

Philip Theophrastus Bombastus of Hoenhaim, or Paracelsus, born as he saith himself in the wildernesse of Helvetia, *Anno* 1493. of the noble and ancient family of the Hoenhaims. But Thomas Erastus making strict enquiry after his pedigree found none of his name or kindred in that place. Yet it is fit so great a Chymist should make himself to be of noble extraction: And let us believe him to be of high descent, as perchance born on some mountain in Switzerland.

As for his Education, he himself boasts that he lived in most Universities of Europe; surely rather as a traveller then a student, and a vagrant then a traveller. Yea some will not allow him so much, and one who hath exactly measured the length of his life, though crowding his pretended travells very close, finds not room enough for them. But 'tis too ridiculous what a Scholar of his relates, that he lived ten years in Arabia to get learning, and conversed in Greece with the Athenian Philosophers. Whereas in that age Arabia the Happy was accursed with Bar-barisme, and Athens grown a stranger to her self;

both which places being then subjected to the Turks, the very ruines of all learning were ruin'd there. Thus we see how he better knew to act his part, then to lay his Scene, and had not Chronologie enough to tell the clock of time, when and where to place his lies to make them like truth.

The first five & twenty years of his age he lived very civilly; being thirty years old he came to Basill, just at the alteration of Religion, when many Papists were expell'd the University, and places rather wanted Professours, then Professours places. Here by the favour of Oecolampadius he was admitted to reade Physick, & for two years behaved himself fairly, till this accident caused his departure. A rich Canon of Basill being sick promised Paracelsus an hundred florens to recover him, which being restored to his health he denied to pay. Paracelsus sues him, is cast in his suit, the Magistrate adjudging him onely an ordinary fee, because the cure was done presently with a few pills. The Physician enraged hereat talked treason against the State in all his discourses, till the nimblenesse of his tongue forc'd the nimblenesse of his feet, and he was fain to fly into Alsatia. Here keeping company with the Gentry of the countrey, he gave himself over to all licentiousnesse: His body was the sea wherein the tide of drunkennesse was ever ebbing and flowing; for by putting his finger in his throat he used to spew out his drink and drunkennesse together, and from that instant date himself sober to return to his cups again. Every moneth he had a new sute, not for pride but necessity; his apparel serving both for wearing and bedding: and having given his clothes many vomits, he gave them to the poore.

Being Codrus over night, he would be Crœsus in the morning, flush of money as if he carried the invisible Indies in his pocket: some suspected the devil was his pursebearer, and that he carried a spirit in the pomel of his sword his constant companion, whilest others maintain that by the heat of the furnace he could ripen any metall into gold.

All the diet he prescribed his patients was this, to eat what, and how often, they thought fitting themselves, and yet he did most strange cures. Like the quicksilver (he so much dealt with) he would never be fixt in one place, or live any where longer then a twelvemoneth: for some observe that by that time the maladies reverted again, which he formerly cured. He gave so strong physick as summoned Nature with all her force to expell the present disease, but the remnant dregs thereof afterwards reinforcing themselves did assault Nature tired out with the violence of her former task, and easily subdued it.

His Scholars brag that the fragments of his learning would feast all the Philosophers in the world, boasting that the gout, the disgrace of Physick, was the honour of Paracelsus, who by curing it removed that scandall from his profession: whereas others say he had little Learning, and lesse Latine. When any asked him the name of an herb he knew not, he would tell them there was no use thereof in Physick; and yet this man would undertake not onely to cure men, but to cure the Art of curing men, and reform Physick it self.

As for his religion, it would as well pose himself as others to tell what it was. He boasted that shortly he would order Luther and the Pope, as well as he had done Galen and Hippocrates. He was never seen to pray, and seldome came to Church. He was not onely skilled in naturall Magick (the utmost bounds whereof border on the suburbs of hell) but is charged to converse constantly with familiars. Guilty he was of all vices but wantonnesse; and I find an honest man his Compurgatour, that he was not given to women; perchance he drank himself into wantonnesse and past it, quenching the fire of his lust by piling fuell too hard and fast upon it.

Boasting that he could make a man immortall, he himself died at fourty seven years in the City of Saltzburg. His Scholars say he was poysoned through the envy (that dark shadow ever waiting on a shining merit) and malice of his adversaries. However his body should have been so fenced with antidotes, that the battery of no poyson might make a breach therein; except we impute it more to his neglect then want of skill, and that rather his own security then his enemies malice brought him to his grave. But it may be he was willing to die, counting a twelvemoneths time enough to stay in one place, and fourty seven years long enough to live in one world. We may more admire that so beastly a drunkard lived so long, then that so skilfull a man died so soon. In a word, He boasted of more then he could do, did more cures seemingly then really, more cures really then lawfully; of more parts then learning, of more fame then parts; a better Physician then a man, and a better Chirurgeon then Physician.

Chap. 4

The Controversiall Divine

HE is Truths Champion to defend her against all adversaries, Atheists, Hereticks, Schismaticks, and Erroneous persons whatsoever. His sufficiency appears in Opposing, Answering, Moderating, and Writing.

He engageth both his judgement, and affections in opposing of falsehood. Not like countrey Fencers, who play onely to make sport, but like Duellers indeed, at it for life and limbe; chiefly if the question be of large prospect, and great concernings, he is zealous in the quarrell. Yet some, though their judgement weigh down on one side, the beam of their affections stands so even, they care not which part prevails.

In opposing a truth, he dissembles himself her foe, to be her better friend. Wherefore he counts himself the greatest conquerour when Truth hath taken him captive. With Joseph having sufficiently sifted the matter in a disguise, he discovereth himself, *I am Joseph your brother*, and then throws away his visard. Dishonest they, who though the debt be satisfied will never give up the bond, but continue wrangling, when the objection is answered.

He abstains from all foul and railing language. What? make the Muses, yea the Graces scolds? Such purulent spittle argues exulcerated lungs. Why should there be so much railing about the body of Christ? when there was none about the body of Moses in the Act kept betwixt the devil and Michael the Archangel.

He tyrannizeth not over a weak and undermatch'd Adversary; but seeks rather to cover his weaknesse if he be a modest man. When a Professour pressed an Answerer (a better Christian then a Clerk) with an hard argument, *Reverende Professor* (said he) *ingenue confiteor me non posse respondere huic argumento*. To whom the Professour, *Recte respondes*.

In answering he states the question, and expoundeth the terms thereof. Otherwise the disputants shall end, where they ought to have begun, in differences about words, and be Barbarians each to other, speaking in a Language neither understand. If the Question also be of Historicall cognizanse, he shews the pedigree thereof, who first brew'd it, who first broch'd it, and sends the wandring Errour with a pasport home to the place of its birth.

In taking away an objection he not onely puts by the thrust, but breaks the weapon. Some rather escape then defeat an argument, and though by such an evasion they may shut the mouth of the Opponent, yet may they open the difficulty wider in the hearts of the hearers. But our Answerer either fairly resolves the doubt; or else shews the falsenesse of the argument, by beggering the Opponent to maintain such a fruitfull generation of absurdities, as his argument hath begotten; or lastly returns and retorts it back upon him again. The first way unties the knot; the second cuts it asunder; the third whips the Opponent with the knot himself tyed. Sure 'tis more honour to be a clear Answerer, then a cunning Opposer, because the latter takes advantage of mans ignorance, which is ten times more then his knowledge.

What his answers want in suddennesse they have in

solidity. Indeed the speedy answer addes lustre to the disputation, and honour to the disputant; yet he makes good payment, who though he cannot presently throw the money out of his pocket, yet will pay it, if but going home to unlock his chest. Some that are not for speedy may be for sounder performance. When Melanchthon at the disputation of Ratisbon was pressed with a shrewd argument by Ecchius, I will answer thee, said he, to morrow. Nay, said Ecchius, do it now or it's nothing worth. Yea, said Melanchthon, I seek the Truth, and not mine own Credit, and therefore it will be as good if I answer thee to morrow by Gods assistance.

In moderating he sides with the Answerer, if the Answerer sides with the truth. But if he be conceited, & opinioned of his own sufficiency, he lets him swound before he gives him any hot water. If a Paradox-monger, loving to hold strange yea dangerous Opinions, he counts it charity to suffer such a one to be beaten without mercy, that he may be weaned from his wilfulnesse. For the main, he is so a staff to the Answerer, that he makes him stand on his own legs.

In writing, his Latine is pure, so farre as the subject will allow. For those who are to climbe the Alpes are not to expect a smooth and even way. True it is that Schoolmen, perceiving that fallacy had too much covert under the nap of flourishing Language, used thredbare Latine on purpose, and cared not to trespasse on Grammar, and tread down the fences thereof to avoid the circuit of words, and to go the nearest way to expresse their conceits. But our Divine though he useth barbarous School-terms, which like standers are fixt to the controversie, yet in his moveable Latine passages, and digressions his style is pure and elegant.

He affects clearnesse and plainnesse in all his writings. Some mens heads are like the world before God said unto it, *Fiat lux*. These dark-lanterns may shine to themselves, and understand their own conceits, but no body else can have light from them. Thus Matthias Farinator Professour at Vienna, assisted with some other learned men, as the Times then went, was thirty years making a book of applying Plato's, Aristotle's, and Galen's rules in Philosophy, to Christ and his Prophets, and 'tis call'd *Lumen animæ; quo tamen nihil est caliginosius, labore magno, sed ridiculo, & inani.* But this obscurity is worst when affected, when they do as Persius, of whom one saith, *Legi voluit quæ scripsit, intelligi noluit quae legerentur*. Some affect this darknesse, that they may be accounted profound, whereas one is not bound to believe that all the water is deep that is muddy.

He is not curious in searching matters of no moment. Captain Martin Frobisher fetcht from the farthest northern Countries a ships lading of minerall stones (as he thought) which afterwards were cast out to mend the high wayes. Thus are they served, and misse their hopes, who long seeking to extract hidden mysteries out of nice questions, leave them off, as uselesse at last. Antoninus Pius, for his desire to search to the least differences, was called *Cumini sector*, the Carver of cumine seed. One need not be so accurate: for as soon shall one scowr the spots out of the moon, as all ignorance out of man. When Eunomius the Heretick vaunted that he knew God and his divinity, *S.* Basil gravells him in 21 questions about the body of an ant or pismire: so dark is mans understanding. I wonder therefore at the boldnesse of some, who as if they were Lord Marshalls of the Angels place them in ranks and files. Let us not believe them here, but rather go to heaven to confute them.

He neither multiplies needlesse, nor compounds necessary Controversies. Sure they light on a labour in vain, who seek to make a bridge of reconciliation over the μέγα χάσμα betwixt Papists and Protestants; for though we go 99 steps, they (I mean their Church) will not come one to give us a meeting. And as for the offers of Clara's and private men (besides that they seem to be more of the nature of baits then gifts) they may make large profers, without any Commission to treat, and so the Romish Church not bound to pay their promises. In Merionethshire in Wales there are high mountains, whose hanging tops come so close together that shepherds on the tops of severall hills may audibly talk together, yet will it be a dayes journey for their bodies to meet, so vast is the hollownesse of the vallies betwixt them. Thus upon sound search shall we find a grand distance and remotenesse betwixt Popish and Protestant tenents to reconcile them, which at the first view may seem near, and tending to an accomodation.

He is resolute and stable in fundamentall points of Religion. These are his fixed poles, and axletree about which he moves, whilest they stand unmoveable. Some sail so long on the Sea of controversies, toss'd up and down, to and fro, *Pro* and *Con*, that the very ground to them seems to move, and their judgements grow scepticall and unstable in the most settled points

of Divinity. When he cometh to Preach, especially
if to a plain Auditory, with the Paracelsians he extracts
an oyl out of the driest and hardest bodies, and knowing that knotty timber is unfit to build with, he edifies
people with easie and profitable matter.

CHAP. 5

*The life of D*ʳ *WHITAKER*

William Whitaker born at Holm in the County of
Lancaster of good parentage, especially by his mothers
side, allied to two worshipfull families. His reverend
unckle, Alexander Nowell, Dean of S. Pauls (the first
fruits of the English Confessours in the dayes of
Queen Marie, who after her death first return'd into
England from beyond the Seas) took him young from
his parents, sent him first to Pauls School, thence to
Trinity Colledge in Cambridge; where he so profited
in his studies, that he gave great promises of his
future perfection.

I passe by his youthfull exercises, never striving for
the garland, but he wonne and wore it away. His
prime appearing to the world, was when he stood for
the Professours place against two Competitours, in
age farre his superiours. But the seven Electours in
the Universitie who were to choose the Emperour of
the Schools, preferring a golden head before silver
hairs, conferr'd the place on Whitaker; and the strict
form of their Election hath no room for corruption.
He so well acquitted himself in the place that he
answered expectation, the strongest opponent in all

disputes and lectures, and by degrees taught envie to admire him.

By this time the Papists began to assault him, and the Truth. First Campian, one fitter for a Trumpeter then a Souldier, whose best ability was that he could boast in good Latine, being excellent at the flat hand of Rhetorick (which rather gives pats then blows) but he could not bend his fist to dispute. Whitaker both in writing and disputing did teach him, that it was easier to make then maintain a challenge against our Church; and in like manner he handled both Duræus, and Sanders, who successively undertook the same cause, solidly confuting their arguments.

But these Teazers, rather to rouze then pinch the Game, onely made Whitaker find his spirits. The fiercest dog is behind even Bellarmine himself, a great scholar, and who wanted nothing but a good cause to defend, and generally writing ingeniously, using sometimes slenting, seldome down-right railing. Whitaker gave him all fair quarter, stating the question betwixt them, yielding all which the other in reason could ask, and agreeing on terms to fall out with him, plaid fairly but fiercely on him, till the other forsook the field.

Bellarmine had no mind to reinforce his routed arguments, but rather consigned over that service to a new Generall, Stapleton an English man: He was born the same yeare and moneth wherein S^r. Thomas More was beheaded, an observation little lesse then mysticall with the Papists, as if God had substituted him to grow up in the room of the other for the support of the Catholick cause. If Whitaker in answering him put more gall then usuall into his ink, Stapleton (whose mouth was as foul as his cause) first infected him with bitternesse: and none will blame a man for arming his hands with hard and rough gloves, who is to meddle with bryers and brambles.

Thus they baited him constantly with fresh dogs: None that ran at him once desired a second course at him; and as one observes, *Cum nullo hoste unquam conflixit, quem non fudit & fugavit.*

He filled the Chair with a gracefull presence, so that one needed not to do with him as Luther did with Melanchthon when he first heard him reade, abstract the opinion and sight of his stature and person, lest the meannesse thereof should cause an undervaluing of him: for our Whitakers person carried with it an excellent port. His style was manly for the strength, maidenly for the modesty, and elegant for the phrase thereof; shewing his skill in spinning a fine thred out of coarse wool, for such is controversiall matter. He had by his second wife, a modest woman, eight children. It being true of him also, what is said of the famous Lawyer Andreas Tiraquillus, *singulis annis singulos libros & liberos Reipublicæ dedit.*

My Father hath told me, that he often wished that he might lose so much Learning as he had gotten in after-supper studies, on condition he might gain so much strength as he had lost thereby. Indeed his body was strongly built for the naturall temper, and well repair'd by his temperate diet and recreations; but first he foundred the foundation of this house by immoderate study, and at last the roof was set on fire by a hot disease.

The unhappy controversie was then started, Whether justifying faith may be lost. And this thorny question would not suffer our Nightingale to sleep. He was sent for up by Arch-bishop Whitgift to the conference at Lambeth, after which returning home, unseasonable riding, late studying, and night-watching brought him to a burning-fever, to which his body was naturally disposed, as appeared by the mastery of rednesse in his complexion. Thus lost he the health of his body, in maintaining, That the health of the soul could not be lost. All agreed that he should be let bloud; which might then easily have been done, but was deferred by the fault of some about him, till it was too late. Thus, when God intends to cut a mans life off, his dearest friends by dangerous involuntarie mistakes shall bring the knife. He died in the 47. yeare of his age, *Anno Dom.* 1595. and in S. Johns Colledge (whereof he was Master) was solemnly interred, with the grief of the University, and whole Church of God.

Chap. 6

The true Church Antiquary

He is a traveller into former times, whence he hath learnt their language and fashions. If he meets with an old manuscript, which hath the mark worn out of its mouth, and hath lost the date, yet he can tell the age thereof either by the phrase or character.

He baits at middle Antiquity, but lodges not till he comes at that which is ancient indeed. Some scoure off the rust of old inscriptions into their own souls, cankering themselves with superstition, having read so often *Orate pro anima*, that at last they fall a praying for the departed; and they more lament the ruine of Monasteryes, then the decay and ruine of Monks lives, degenerating from their ancient piety and painfulnesse. Indeed a little skill in Antiquity inclines a man to Popery; but depth in that study brings him about again to our religion. A Nobleman who had heard of the extreme age of one dwelling not farre off, made a journey to visit him, and finding an aged person sitting in the chimney-corner, addressed himself unto him with admiration of his age, till his mistake was rectified: for, *Oh S^r*, (said the young-old man) *I am not he whom you seek for, but his sonne; my father is farther off in the field*. The same errour is daily comitted by the Romish Church, adoring the reverend brow and gray hairs of some ancient Ceremonyes, perchance but of some seven or eight hundred years standing in the Church, and mistake these for their fathers, of farre greater age in the Primitive times.

He desires to imitate the ancient Fathers, as well in their Piety, as in their Postures. Not onely conforming his hands and knees, but chiefly his heart to their pattern. O the holinesse of their living and painfulnesse of their preaching! how full were they of mortified thoughts, and heavenly meditations! Let us not make the ceremoniall part of their lives onely Canonicall, and the morall part thereof altogether Apocrypha, imitating their devotion not in the finenesse of the stuff, but onely in the fashion of the making.

He carefully marks the declination of the Church from the Primitive purity. Observing how sometimes humble devotion was contented to lie down, whilest

proud superstition got on her back. Yea not onely
Frederick the Emperour, but many a godly Father
some hundreds of years before held the Pope's stirrop,
and by their well-meaning simplicity gave occasion
to his future greatnesse. He takes notice how their
Rhetoricall hyperboles were afterwards accounted the
just measure of dogmaticall truths; How plain people
took them at their word in their funerall apostrophes
to the dead; How praying for the departed brought
the fuell, under which after-ages kindled the fire of
Purgatory; How one Ceremony begat another, there
being no bounds in will-worship, wherewith one may
sooner be wearied then satisfied; the inventours of
new Ceremonyes endeavouring to supply in number,
what their conceits want in solidity; How mens souls
being in the full speed and career of the Historicall
use of Pictures could not stop short, but must lash out
into superstition, How the Fathers vailing their bon-
nets to Rome in civill courtesie, when making honour-
able mention thereof, are interpreted by modern
Papists to have done it in adoration of the idole of
the Popes infallibility. All these things he ponders
in his heart, observing both the times and places,
when and where they happened.

*He is not zealous for the introducing of old uselesse
Ceremonies.* The mischief is, some that are most violent to bring such in, are most negligent to preach the
cautions in using them; and simple people, like Children in eating of fish, swallow bones and all to their
danger of choking. Besides, what is observed of
horse-hairs, that lying nine dayes in water they turn
to snakes; so some Ceremonies though dead at first,
in continuance of time quicken, get stings, and may

do much mischief, especially if in such an age wherein the meddling of some have justly awaked the jealousie of all. When many Popish tricks are abroad in the countrey; if then men meet with a Ceremony which is a stranger, especially if it can give but a bad account of it self, no wonder if the watch take it up for one on suspicion.

He is not peremptory but conjecturall in doubtfull matters. Not forcing others to his own opinion, but leaving them to their own libertie; not filling up all with his own conjectures to leave no room for other men: nor tramples he on their credits, if in them he finds slips and mistakes. For here our souls have but one eye (the Apostle faith, *we know in part*) be not proud if that chance to come athwart thy seeing side, which meets with the blind side of another.

He thankfully acknowledgeth those by whom he hath profited. Base natured they, who when they have quenched their own thirst, stop up, at least muddy, the fountain. But our Antiquary, if he be not the first Founder of a commendable conceit, contents himself to be a Benefactour to it in clearing and adorning it.

He affects not phancy-full singularity in his behaviour: Nor cares he to have a proper mark in writing of words, to disguise some peculiar letter from the ordinary character. Others, for fear travellers should take no notice that skill in Antiquity dwells in such an head, hang out an antique hat for the signe, or use some obsolete garb in their garments, gestures, or discourse.

He doth not so adore the Ancients as to despise the Modern. Grant them but dwarfs, yet stand they on giants shoulders, and may see the further. Sure, as

stout champions of Truth follow in the rere, as ever
march'd in the front. Besides, as one excellently observes, *Antiquitas seculi juventus mundi*. These times
are the ancient times, when the world is ancient; and
not those which we count ancient *ordine retrogrado*,
by a computation backwards from our selves.

Chap. 7

The generall Artist

I know the generall cavill against generall learning is
this, that *aliquis in omnibus est nullus in singulis*. He
that sips of many arts, drinks of none. However we
must know, that all learning, which is but one grand
Science, hath so homogeneall a body, that the parts
thereof do with a mutuall service relate to, and com-
municate strength and lustre each to other. Our
Artist knowing language to be the key of learning,
thus begins.

*His tongue being but one by nature he gets cloven by
art and industry*. Before the confusion of Babel, all
the world was one continent in language; since divided
into severall tongues, as severall ilands. Grammer is
the ship, by benefit whereof we passe from one to
another, in the learned languages generally spoken in
no countrey. His mother-tongue was like the dull
musick of a monochord, which by study he turns
into the harmony of severall instruments.

He first gaineth skill in the Latine and Greek tongues.
On the credit of the former alone, he may trade in
discourse over all Christendome: But the Greek,

though not so generally spoken, is known with no lesse profit, and more pleasure. The joynts of her compounded words are so naturally oyled, that they run nimbly on the tongue; which makes them though long never tedious, because significant. Besides, it is full and stately in sound: onely it pities our Artist to see the vowels therein rackt in pronouncing them, hanging oftentimes one way by their native force, and haled another by their accents which countermand them.

Hence he proceeds to the Hebrew, the mother-tongue of the world. More pains then quicknesse of wit is required to get it, and with daily exercise he continues it. Apostacy herein is usuall to fall totally from the language by a little neglect. As for the Arabick, and other Orientall languages, he rather makes sallies and incursions into them, then any solemn sitting down before them.

Then he applies his study to Logick, and Ethicks. The latter makes a mans soul mannerly & wise; but as for Logick, that is the armory of reason, furnished with all offensive and defensive weapons. There are Syllogismes, long swords; Enthymems, short daggers; Dilemma's, two-edged swords that cut on both sides; Sorites, chain-shot: And for the defensive, Distinctions, which are shields; Retortions, which are targets with a pike in the midst of them, both to defend and oppose. From hence he raiseth his studies to the knowledge of Physicks, the great hall of Nature, and Metaphysicks the closet thereof; and is carefull not to wade therein so farre, till by subtle distinguishing of notions he confounds himself.

He is skilfull in Rhetorick, which gives a speech colour, as Logick doth favour, and both together beauty. Though some condemne Rhetorick as the mother of lies, speaking more then the truth in Hyperboles, lesse in her Miosis, otherwise in her metaphors, contrary in her ironies; yet is there excellent use of all these, when disposed of with judgement. Nor is he a stranger to Poetry, which is musick in words; nor to Musick, which is poetry in sound: both excellent sauce, but they have liv'd and died poore, that made them their meat.

Mathematicks he moderately studieth to his great contentment. Using it as ballast for his soul, yet to fix it not to stall it; nor suffers he it to be so unmannerly as to justle out other arts. As for judiciall Astrology (which hath the least judgement in it) this vagrant hath been whipt out of all learned corporations. If our Artist lodgeth her in the out-rooms of his soul for a night or two, it is rather to heare then believe her relations.

Hence he makes his progresse into the study of History. Nestor, who lived three ages, was accounted the wisest man in the world. But the Historian may make himself wise by living as many ages as have past since the beginning of the world. His books enable him to maintain discourse, who besides the stock of his own experience may spend on the common purse of his reading. This directs him in his life, so that he makes the shipwracks of others sea-marks to himself; yea accidents which others start from for their strangenes, he welcomes as his wonted acquaintance, having found presidents for them formerly. Without History a mans soul is purblind, seeing onely the things which almost touch his eyes.

He is well seen in Chronology, without which History

is but an heap of tales. If by the Laws of the land he is counted a Naturall, who hath not wit enough to tell twenty, or to tell his age; he shall not passe with me for wise in learning, who cannot tell the age of the world, and count hundreds of years: I mean not so critically, as to solve all doubts arising thence; but that he may be able to give some tolerable account thereof. He is also acquainted with Cosmography, treating of the world in whole joynts; with Chorography, shredding it into countries; and with Topography, mincing it into particular places.

Thus taking these Sciences in their generall latitude, he hath finished the round circle or golden ring of the arts; onely he keeps a place for the diamond to be set in, I mean for that predominant profession of Law, Physick, Divinity, or State-policie, which he intends for his principall Calling hereafter.

Chap. 8

The life of Julius Scaliger

I know my choice herein is liable to much exception. Some will make me the pattern of ignorance, for making this Scaliger the pattern of the generall Artist, whose own sonne Joseph might have been his father in many arts. But all things considered, the choice will appear well advised, even in such variety of examples. Yet let him know that undertakes to pick out the best ear amongst an acre of wheat, that he shall leave as good if not a better behind him, then that which he chooseth.

He was born *Anno* 1484. in Italie, at the Castle of
Ripa upon lacus Benacus, now called *Lago di Garda*,
of the illustrious and noble family of the Scaligers,
Princes, for many hundreds of years, of Verona, till
at last the Venetians outed them of their ancient
inheritance. Being about eleven years old, he was
brought to the Court of Maximilian Emperour of
Germany, where for seventeen years together he was
taught learning, and military discipline. I passe by
his valiant performances achieved by him, save that
this one action of his is so great and strong, it cannot
be kept in silence, but will be recorded.

In the cruel battel at Ravenna betwixt the Emperour
and the French, he not onely bravely fetch'd off the
dead bodies of Benedictus and Titus his father and
brother, but also with his own hands rescued the
Eagle (the standard Imperiall) which was taken by
the enemies. For which his prowesse Maximilian
knighted him, and with his own hands put on him the
golden spurres, and chain, the badges of knight-hood.

Amidst these his Martiall employments he made
many a clandestine match with the Muses, and whilest
he expected the tides and returns of businesse, he
fill'd up the empty places of leisure with his studies.
Well did the Poets feigne Pallas Patronesse of arts
and armes, there being ever good intelligence betwixt
the two Professions, and as it were but a narrow cut to
ferry over out of one into the other. At last Scaliger
sounded a retreat to himself from the warres, and
wholly applyed himself to his book, especially after
his wandring life was fixed by marriage unto the
beautifull Andietta Lobeiaca, with whom he lived at
Agin, near Montpeliar in France.

His Latine was twice refined, and most criticall, as appears by his own writings, and notes on other Authours. He was an accurate Grecian, yet began to study it, when well nigh fourty years old, when a mans tongue is too stiff to bow to words. What a torture was it to him who flowed with streams of matter then to learn words, yea letters, drop by drop? But nothing was unconquerable to his pains, who had a golden wit in an iron body. Let his book of Subtilties witnesse his profound skill in Logick, and Naturall Philosophy.

His skill in Physick was as great, as his practice therein was happy; in so much that he did many strange and admirable cures. Heare how a noble and learned pen doth commend him:

Non hunc fefellit ulla vis recondita
Salubris herbæ, saltibus si quam aviis
Celat nivosus Caucasus, seu quam procul
Riphæa duro contigit rupes gelu.
Hic jamque spectantes ad orcum non semel
Animas repressit victor, & membris suis
Hærere succis compulit felicibus,
Nigrique avaras Ditis elusit manus.

On snowy Caucasus there grew no root
Of secret power, but he was privy to 't;
On cold Riphean hills no simple grew,
But he the force thereof and virtue knew.
Wherewith (apply'd by his successefull art)
Such sullen souls as would this world depart,
He forc'd still in their bodies to remain,
And from deaths doore fetch'd others back again.

As for his skill in Physiognomy, it was wonderfull. I know some will say, that cannot be read in mens

faces which was never wrote there, and that he that
seeks to find the disposition of mens souls in the
figures of their bodies, looks for letters on the back-
side of the book. Yet is it credibly averred that he
never look'd on his infant-sonne Audectus but with
grief, as sorrow-struck with some sad signe of ill successe he saw in his face: which child at last was found
stifled in bed with the embraces of his nurse being
fast asleep.

In Mathematicks he was no Archimedes, though
he shewed his skill therein with the best advantage,
and stood therein on his tiptoes, that his learning
might seem the taller.

But in Poetry his over-measure of skill might make
up this defect, as is attested by his book *de Arte
Poetica*. Yet his own Poems are harsh, and unsmooth,
(as if he rather snorted then slept on Parnassus) and
they sound better to the brain then the eare. Indeed his censure in Poetry was incomparable; but he
was more happy in repairing of Poems then in building
them from the ground, which speaks his judgement
to be better then his invention.

What shall I speak of his skill in History? whose
own actions were a sufficient History. He was excellently vers'd in the passages of the world, both modern
and ancient. Many modern languages, which departed
from Babel in a confusion, met in his mouth in a
method, being skilfull in the Sclavonick tongue, the
Hungarian, Dutch, Italian, Spanish, and French.

But these his excellent parts were attended with
prodigious pride; and he had much of the humour of
the Ottomans in him, to kill all his brethren, and cry
down all his equalls, which were corrivalls with him

in the honour of arts, which was his principall quarrell
with Cardan. Great was his spight at Erasmus, the
morning-starre of learning, and one by whom Julius
himself had profited, though afterwards he sought to
put out that candle whereat he had lighted his own.
In the bickering betwixt them, Erasmus pluckt Scaliger
by the long locks of his immoderate boasting, and
touched him to the quick (a proud man lies pat for a
jeering mans hand to hit) yea Erasmus was a badger in
his jeeres, where he did bite he would make his teeth
meet. Nor came Scaliger behind him in railing. However afterward Scaliger repented of his bitternesse,
and before his death was reconciled unto him.

Thus his learning, being in the circuit of arts,
spread so wide, no wonder if it lay thinne in some
places. His parts were nimble, that starting so late
he overtook, yea overran his equalls: so that we may
safely conclude that making abatement for his military
avocations, and late applying himself to study, scarce
any one is to be preferred before him for generality
of humane learning. He died *Anno* 1558. in the 75.
yeare of his age.

Chap. 9

The faithfull Minister

We suppose him not brought up by hand onely in his
own countrey studies, but that he hath suckt of his
Mother University, and throughly learnt the arts:
Not as S. Rumball, who is said to have spoken as
soon as he was born, doth he preach as soon as he is
Matriculated. Conceive him now a Graduate in arts,

and entred into orders, according to the solemn form of the Church of England, and presented by some Patrone to a pastorall charge, or place equivalent, and then let us see how well he dischargeth his office.

He endeavours to get the generall love and good will of his parish. This he doth not so much to make a benefit of them, as a benefit for them, that his ministry may be more effectuall; otherwise he may preach his own heart out, before he preacheth any thing into theirs. The good conceit of the Physician is half a cure, and his practice will scarce be happy where his person is hated; yet he humours them not in his Doctrine to get their love: for such a spanniel is worse then a dumbe dog. He shall sooner get their good will by walking uprightly, then by crouching and creeping. If pious living and painfull labouring in his calling will not win their affections, he counts it gain to lose them. As for those which causelessely hate him, he pities and prayes for them: and such there will be; I should suspect his preaching had no salt in it, if no gald horse did winse.

He is strict in ordering his conversation. As for those who clense blurres with blotted fingers, they make it the worse. It was said of one who preach'd very well, & liv'd very ill, *That when he was out of the Pulpit, it was pity he should ever go into it, & when he was in the Pulpit, it was pity he should ever come out of it*: But our Minister lives Sermons. And yet I deny not but dissolute men, like unskilfull horsemen which open a gate on the wrong side, may by the virtue of their office open heaven for others, and shut themselves out.

His behaviour towards his people is grave and courteous. Not too austere and retired; which is laid to

the charge of good Mr Hooper the martyr, that his
rigidnesse frighted people from consulting with him.
Let your light (saith Christ) *shine before men*; whereas
over reservednesse makes the brightest virtue burn
dimme. Especially he detesteth affected gravity
(which is rather on men then in them) whereby some
belie their register-book, antedate their age to seem
farre older then they are, and plait and set their brows
in an affected sadnesse. Whereas S. Anthony the Monk
might have been known among hundreds of his order
by his cheerfull face, he having ever (though a most
mortified man) a merry countenance.

*He doth not clash Gods ordinances together about pre-
cedency*. Not making odious comparisons betwixt
Prayer and Preaching, Preaching and Catechising,
Publick prayer and Private, Premeditate prayer and
Ex tempore. When at the taking of new Carthage in
Spain two Souldiers contended about the Murall
crown (due to him who first climbed the walls) so
that the whole army was thereupon in danger of divi-
sion, Scipio the Generall said, He knew that they both
got up the wall together, and so gave the Scaling
crown to them both. Thus our Minister compounds
all controversies betwixt Gods ordinances, by praysing
them all, practising them all, and thanking God for
them all. He counts the reading of Common-prayers
to prepare him the better for preaching; and as one
said, if he did first toll the bell on one side, it made it
afterwards ring out the better in his Sermons.

*He carefully Catechiseth his people in the elements of
religion*. Except he hath (a rare thing) a flock without
lambs, all of old sheep; and yet even Luther did not
scorn to professe himself *Discipulum Catechismi*, a

scholar of the Catechisme. By this Catechising the Gospel first got ground of Popery; and let not our Religion now grown rich be ashamed of that which first gave it credit and set it up, lest the Jesuites beat us at our own weapon. Through the want of this Catechising many which are well skilled in some dark out-corners of Divinity have lost themselves in the beaten road thereof.

He will not offer to God of that which costs him nothing; but takes pains aforehand for his Sermons. Demosthenes never made any oration on the sudden; yea being called upon he never rose up to speak, except he had well studied the matter: and he was wont to say, *That he shewed how he honoured and reverenced the people of Athens because he was carefull what he spake unto them*. Indeed if our Minister be surprised with a sudden occasion, he counts himself rather to be excused then commended, if premeditating onely the bones of his Sermon he clothes it with flesh *ex tempore*. As for those, whose long custome hath made preaching their nature, that they can discourse Sermons without study, he accounts their examples rather to be admired then imitated.

Having brought his Sermon into his head, he labours to bring it into his heart, before he preaches it to his people. Surely that preaching which comes from the soul most works on the soul. Some have questioned ventriloquie, when men strangely speak out of their bellies, whether it can be done lawfully or no: might I coin the word *cordiloquie*, when men draw the doctrines out of their hearts, sure all would count this lawfull and commendable.

He chiefly reproves the raigning sins of the time, and

place he lives in. We may observe that our Saviour never inveighed against Idolatry, Usury, Sabbath-breaking amongst the Jews; not that these were not sins, but they were not practised so much in that age, wherein wickednesse was spun with a finer thred: and therefore Christ principally bent the drift of his preaching against spirituall Pride, Hypocrisie, and Traditions then predominant amongst the people. Also our Minister confuteth no old Heresies which time hath confuted; nor troubles his Auditory with such strange, hideous cases of Conscience, that it is more hard to find the case then the resolution. In publick reproving of sinne, he ever whips the vice, and spares the person.

He doth not onely move the bread of life, and tosse it up and down in generalities, but also breaks it into particular directions: drawing it down to cases of Conscience, that a man may be warranted in his particular actions, whether they be lawfull or not. And he teacheth people their lawfull liberty as well as their restraints and prohibitions; for amongst men it is as ill taken to turn back favours, as to disobey commands.

The places of Scripture he quotes are pregnant and pertinent. As for heaping up of many quotations, it smacks of a vain ostentation of memory. Besides, it is as impossible that the hearer should profitably retain them all, as that the preacher hath seriously perused them all: yea, whilest the auditours stop their attention, and stoop down to gather an impertinent quotation, the Sermon runs on, and they lose more substantiall matter.

His similes and illustrations are alwayes familiar, never

contemptible. Indeed reasons are the pillars of the
fabrick of a Sermon, but similitudes are the windows
which give the best light. He avoids such stories
whose mention may suggest bad thoughts to the
auditours, and will not use a light comparison to
make thereof a grave application, for fear lest his
poyson go farther then his antidote.

*He provideth not onely wholsome but plentifull food
for his people*. Almost incredible was the painfulnesse
of Baronius, the compiler of the voluminous Annals
of the Church, who for thirty years together preached
three or foure times aweek to the people. As for our
Minister, he preferreth rather to entertain his people
with wholsome cold meat which was on the table
before, then with that which is hot from the spit, raw
and half roasted. Yet in repetition of the same
Sermon, every edition hath a new addition, if not
of new matter of new affections. *Of whom*, saith
S. Paul, *we have told you often, and now we tell you
weeping*.

*He makes not that wearisome, which should ever be
welcome*. Wherefore his Sermons are of an ordinary
length except on an extraordinary occasion. What a
gift had John Haselbach, Professour at Vienna, in
tediousnesse? who being to expound the Prophet Esay
to his auditours read twenty one years on the first
Chapter, and yet finished it not.

*He counts the success of his Ministry the greatest pre-
ferment*. Yet herein God hath humbled many painfull
pastours, in making them to be clouds to rain, not
over Arabia the happy but over the stonie or desert:
so that they may complain with the Herdsman in the
Poet,

Heu mihi, quam pingui macer est mihi taurus in arvo?
>My starveling bull,
>Ah woe is me,
>In pasture full,
>How lean is he?

Yet such Pastours may comfort themselves that great is their reward with God in heaven, who measures it not by their successe but endeavours. Besides, though they see not, their people may feel benefit by their Ministry. Yea the preaching of the Word in some places is like the planting of woods, where though no profit is received for twenty years together, it comes afterwards. And grant, that God honours thee not to build his temple in thy parish, yet thou maist with David provide metall and materialls for Solomon thy successour to build it with.

To sick folks he comes sometimes before he is sent for, as counting his vocation a sufficient calling. None of his flock shall want the extreme unction of Prayer and Counsell. Against the Communion especially he endeavours that Janus his temple be shut in the whole parish, and that all be made friends.

He is never plaintiff in any suit but to be rights defendant. If his dues be detained from him, he grieves more for his parishioners bad conscience then his own damage. He had rather suffer ten times in his profit, then once in his title, where not onely his person, but posterity is wronged: And then he proceeds fairly and speedily to a tryall, that he may not vex and weary others, but right himself. During his suit he neither breaks off nor slacks offices of courtesie to his adversary; yea though he loseth his suit, he will not also lose his charity. Chiefly he is respectfull to his Patrone, that as he presented him freely to his living, so he constantly presents his Patrone in his prayers to God.

He is moderate in his tenets and opinions. Not that he gilds over lukewarmnesse in matters of moment with the title of discretion, but withall he is carefull not to entitle violence in indifferent and in concerning matters to be zeal. Indeed men of extraordinary tallnesse, (though otherwise little deserving) are made porters to lords, & those of unusuall littlenesse are made ladies dwarfs, whilest men of moderate stature may want masters. Thus many notorious for extremities may find favourers to preferre them, whilest moderate men in the middle truth may want any to advance them. But what saith the Apostle? *If in this life onely we had hope we are of all men the most miserable.*

He is sociable and willing to do any courtesie for his neighbour Ministers. He willingly communicates his knowledge unto them. Surely the gifts and graces of Christians lay in common, till base envy made the first enclosure. He neither slighteth his inferiours; nor repineth at those who in parts and credit are above him. He loveth the company of his neighbour Ministers. Sure as ambergreece is nothing so sweet in it self, as when it is compounded with other things; so both godly and learned men are gainers by communicating themselves to their neighbours.

He is carefull in the discreet ordering of his own family. A good Minister and a good father may well agree together. When a certain Frenchman came to visit Melanchthon, he found him in his stove with one hand dandling his child in the swadling-clouts, and in the other hand holding a book and reading it. Our Minister also is as hospitable as his estate will permit, and makes every almes two by his cheerfull giving it. He loveth also to live in a well-repaired house, that he may serve God therein more cheerfully. A Clergieman who built his house from the ground wrote in it this counsell to his successour,

If thou dost find an house built to thy mind
Without thy cost,
Serve thou the more God and the poore;
My labour is not lost.

Lying on his deathbed he bequeaths to each of his parishioners his precepts and example for a legacie: and they in requitall erect every one a monument for him in their hearts. He is so farre from that base jealousie that his memory should be outshined by a brighter successour, and from that wicked desire that his people may find his worth by the worthlesnesse of him that succeeds, that he doth heartily pray to God to provide them a better Pastour after his decease. As for outward estate, he commonly lives in too bare pasture to die fat: It is well if he hath gathered any flesh, being more in blessing then bulk.

Chap. 10

The life of Mr Perkins

William Perkins, born at Marston nigh Coventry in Warwickshire, was afterwards brought up in Christ-Colledge in Cambridge, where he so well profited in his studies that he got the grounds of all liberall Arts, and in the 24. of Queen Elizabeth was chosen fellow of that Colledge, the same yeare wherein Doctour Andrew Willet (one of admirable industry) and Doctour Richard Clark (whose learned Sermons commend him to posterity) were elected into the same Society.

There goeth an uncontroll'd tradition, that Perkins, when a young scholar, was a great studier of Magick, occasioned perchance by his skill in Mathematicks. For ignorant people count all circles above their own sphere to be conjuring, and presently cry out those things are done by black art for which their dimme eyes can see no colour in reason. And in such cases, when they cannot flie up to heaven to make it a Miracle, they fetch it from hell to make it Magick, though it may lawfully be done by naturall causes. True it is he was very wild in his youth till God (the best Chymick who can fix quicksilver it self) gratiously reclaim'd him.

After his entrance into the Ministry, the first beam he sent forth shined to those *which sat in darknesse and the shadow of death*, I mean the prisoners in the castle of Cambridge, people (as generally in such places) living in England out of Christendome, wanting the means of their salvation, bound in their bodies, but too loose in their lives, yea often branded in their flesh, and seared in their consciences. Perkins prevailed so farre with their jaylour, that the prisoners were brought (fetter'd) to the Shire-house hard by, where he preached unto them every Lords day. Thus was the prison his parish, his own Charity his Patron presenting him unto it, and his work was all his wages. Many an Onesimus here he begat, and as the instru-

ment freed the prisoners from the captivity of sinne.
When this began to be known, some of good quality
of the neighbouring parishes became his auditours,
and counted it their feast to feed out of the prisoners
basket. Hence afterwards he became Preacher of
S. Andrews parish in Cambridge, where he continued
to the day of his death.

His Sermons were not so plain but that the piously
learned did admire them, nor so learned but that the
plain did understand them. What was said of Socrates,
That he first humbled the towring speculations of
Philosophers into practice and morality; so our Perkins
brought the schools into the Pulpit, and unshelling
their controversies out of their hard school-terms,
made thereof plain and wholsome meat for his people.
For he had a capacious head with angles winding, and
roomthy enough to lodge all controversiall intricacies;
and, had not preaching diverted him from that way,
he had no doubt attained to eminency therein. An
excellent Chirurgeon he was at joynting of a broken
soul, and at stating of a doubtfull conscience. And
sure in Case-divinity Protestants are defective. For
(save that a Smith or two of late have built them
forges, and set up shop) we go down to our enemies
to sharpen all our instruments, and are beholden to
them for offensive and defensive weapons in Cases of
Conscience.

He would pronounce the word *Damne* with such an
emphasis as left a dolefull Echo in his auditours ears
a good while after. And when Catechist of Christ-
Colledge, in expounding the Commandments, applied
them so home, able almost to make his hearers hearts
fall down, and hairs to stand upright. But in his older

age he altered his voice, and remitted much of his former rigidnesse, often professing that to preach mercie was that proper office of the Ministers of the Gospell.

Some object that his Doctrine, referring all to an absolute decree, hamstrings all industry, and cuts off the sinews of mens endeavours towards salvation. For ascribing all to the wind of Gods spirit, (which bloweth where it listeth) he leaveth nothing to the oars of mans diligence, either to help or hinder to the attaining of happinesse, but rather opens a wide doore to licentious security. Were this the hardest objection against Perkins his doctrine, his own life was a sufficient answer thereunto, so pious, so spotlesse, that Malice was afraid to bite at his credit, into which she knew her teeth could not enter.

He had a rare felicity in speedy reading of books, and as it were but turning them over would give an exact account of all considerables therein. So that as it were riding post thorow an Authour, he took strict notice of all passages, as if he had dwelt on them particularly; perusing books so speedily, one would think he read nothing; so accurately, one would think he read all.

He was of a cheerfull nature and pleasant disposition: Indeed to mere strangers he was reserved and close, suffering them to knock a good while before he would open himself unto them; but on the least acquaintance he was merry and very familiar.

Besides his assiduity in preaching he wrote many books, extant at this day. And pity it was, that he set not forth more of them himself; for though some of his Orphan works lighted on good Guardians, yet all

were not so happy; and indeed no nurse for a child
to the own mother.

He dyed in the 44. yeare of his age of a violent fit
of the stone. It hath been reported that he dyed in
the conflict of a troubled conscience; which admit
were so, had been no wonder. For God sometimes
seemingly leaves his Saints when they leave the world,
plunging them on their death-beds in deep tempta-
tions, and casting their souls down to hell, to rebound
the higher to heaven. Besides, the devil is most busie
on the last day of his Term; and a Tenant to be outed
cares not what mischief he doth. But here was no
such matter. Indeed he alwayes cryed out *Mercy
Mercy*: which some standers by misinterpreted for
despair, as if he felt not Gods favour, because he
call'd for it: whereas Mercy is a Grace which they
hold the fastest, that most catch after it. 'Tis true
that many on lesse reason have expressed more con-
fidence of their future happinesse, and have delivered
themselves in larger speeches concerning the same.
But who could expect a long oration from him, where
every word was accented with pain in so sharp a
disease.

His funeralls were solemnly and sumtuously per-
form'd of the sole charges of Christ-Colledge, which
challenged, as she gave him his breeding, to pay for
his buriall; the University and Town lovingly con-
tending which should expresse more sorrow thereat.
Doctour Mountague, afterwards Bishop of Winchester,
preached his Funerall-Sermon, and excellently dis-
charg'd the place, taking for his Text, *Moses my servant is dead*.

He was of a ruddy complexion, very fat and corpulent, lame of his right hand; and yet this Ehud with a lefthanded pen did stab the Romish Cause, and as one saith,

Dextera quantumvis fuerat tibi manca, docendi
Pollebas mira dexteritate tamen.

Though nature thee of thy right hand bereft,
Right well thou writest with thy hand that's left.

He was born the first, and dyed the last yeare of Queen Elisabeth, so that his life streamed in equall length with her reigne, and they both had their fountains, and falls together.

I must not forget, how his books after his death were translated into most modern Christian languages. For though he excellently improved his talent in the English tongue, yet forreiners thought it but wrapt up in a napkin, whilest folded in an unknown language. Wherefore some translated the main body of his works into French, Dutch, and Italian; and his books speak more tongues, then the Maker ever understood. His *Reformed Catholick* was done into Spanish, and no Spaniard ever since durst take up that gantlet of defiance our Champion cast down: yea their Inquisition rather chose to answer it with tortures, then arguments.

CHAP. II

The good Parishioner

WE will onely describe his Church-reference; his Civill part hath and shall be met with under other Heads. Conceive him to live under such a faithfull Minister as before was character'd, as, either judging charitably that all Pastours are such, or wishing heartily that they were.

Though near to the Church he is not farre from God. Like unto Justus, Acts 18. 8. *One that worshipped God, and his house joyned hard to the Synagogue.* Otherwise if his distance from the church be great, his diligence is the greater to come thither in season.

He is timely at the beginning of Common prayer. Yet as Tullie Charged some dissolute people for being such sluggards that they never saw the sunne rising or setting, as being alwayes up after the one, and abed before the other; so some negligent people never heare prayers begun, or sermon ended: the Confession being past before they come, and the Blessing not come before they are passed away.

In sermon he sets himself to heare God in the Minister. Therefore divesteth he himself of all prejudice, the jaundise in the eyes of the soul presenting colours false unto it. He hearkens very attentively: 'Tis a shame when the Church it self is *Cœmeterium*, wherein the living sleep aboveground as the dead do beneath.

At every Point that concerns himself, he turns down a leaf in his heart; and rejoyceth that Gods word hath peirc'd him, as hoping that whilest his soul smarts it heals. And as it is no manners for him that hath good venison before him, to ask whence it came, but rather fairly to fall to it; so hearing an excellent Sermon, he never enquires whence the Preacher had it, or whether it was not before in print, but falls aboard to practise it.

He accuseth not his Minister of spight for particularizing him. It does not follow that the archer aimed, because the arrow hit. Rather our Parishioner reasoneth thus; If my sinne be notorious, how could the

Minister misse it? if secret, how could he hit it without Gods direction? But foolish hearers make even the bells of Aarons garments *to clink as they think.* And a guilty conscience is like a whirlpool, drawing in all to it self which otherwise would passe by. One, causelessely disaffected to his Minister, complained that he in his last Sermon had personally inveighed against him, and accused him thereof to a grave religious Gentleman in the parish: *Truly*, said the Gentleman, *I had thought in his Sermon he had meant me, for it touched my heart.* This rebated the edge of the others anger.

His Tithes he payes willingly with cheerfulnesse. How many part with Gods portions grudgingly, or else pinch it in the paying. *Decimum*, the Tenth, amongst the Romanes was ever taken for what was best or biggest. It falls out otherwise in paying of Tithes, where the least and leanest are shifted off to make that number.

He hides not himself from any Parish-office which seeks for him. If chosen Churchwarden, he is not busily-idle, rather to trouble then reform, presenting all things but those which he should. If Overseer of the poore, he is carefull the rates be made indifferent (whose inequality oftentimes is more burthensome then the summe) and well disposed of. He measures not peoples wants by their clamorous complaining, and dispenseth more to those that deserve then to them that onely need relief.

He is bountifull in contributing to the repair of Gods house. For though he be not of their opinion, who would have the Churches under the Gospell conform'd to the magnificence of Solomons Temple

(whose porch would serve us for a Church) and adorn
them so gaudily, that devotion is more distracted then
raised, and mens souls rather dazeled, then lightened;
yet he conceives it fitting that such sacred places
should be handsomly and decently maintained: The
rather because the climactericall yeare of many
Churches from their first foundation, may seem to
happen in our dayes; so old, that their ruine is
threatned if not speedily repaired.

*He is respectfull to his Ministers widow and posterity
for his sake.* When the onely daughter of Peter Martyr
was, through the riot and prodigality of her debauched
husband, brought to extreme poverty, the State of
Zurick, out of gratefull remembrance of her Father,
supported her with bountifull maintenance. My
prayers shall be, that Ministers widows, and children
may never stand in need of such relief, and may never
want such relief when they stand in need.

CHAP. 12

The good Patron

That in the Primitive times (though I dare not say
generally in all Churches) if not the sole choyce, at
least the consent of the people was required in appoint-
ing of Ministers, may partly appear out of Scripture,
more plainly out of Cyprian, and is confessed by
reverend Dr Whitgift. These popular elections were
well discharged in those purer times, when men being
scoured with constant persecution had little leasure to
rust with factions, and when there were no baits for

Corruption; the places of Ministers being then of great pains and perill, & small profit. But dissension creeping in, in after-ages (the eyes of common people at the best but dimme through ignorance being wholly blinded with partiality) it may seem their right of election was either devolved to, or assumed of the Bishop of the Dioces, who onely was to appoint Curates in every parish. Afterwards to invite lay-men to build and endow Churches, the Bishops departed with their right to the lay Patrons according to the verse,

Patronum faciunt Dos, Aedificatio, Fundus.

A Patron's he that did endow with lands,

Or built the Church, or on whose ground it stands.

It being conceived reasonable that he who payed the Churches portion, should have the main stroke in providing her an husband. Then came Patronages to be annexed to Mannours, and by sale or descent to passe along with them; nor could any justly complain thereof, if all Patrons were like him we describe.

He counts the Living his to dispose, not to make profit of. He fears more to lapse his conscience, then his Living, fears more the committing then the discovery of Simony.

A Benefice he sometimes giveth speedily, never rashly. Some are long in bestowing them out of state, because they love to have many suiters; others out of covetousnesse will not open their wares till all their chapmen are come together, pretending to take the more deliberation.

He is deaf to importunity, if wanting desert. Yet is he not of the mind of Tamberlane the Scythian King, who never gave Office to any that sought for it: for

desiring proceeds not alwayes from want of deserving;
yea God himself likes well that his favours should be
sued for. Our Patron chiefly respects piety, sufficiency, and promise of painfulnesse, whereby he
makes his election. If he can by the same deed provide for Gods house and his own familie, he counts
it lawfull, but on no terms will preferre his dearest
and nearest sonne or kinsman if unworthy.

*He hates not onely direct simony, or rather Gehazisme,
by the string, but also that which goes about by the bow.*
Ancient Councels present us with severall forms hereof. I find how the Patrons sonnes and nephews were
wont to feed upon the Incumbent, and eat out the
presentation in great banquets and dinners, till at last
the Palentine Councel brought a voyder to such feasts,
and made a canon against them. But the former ages
were bunglers to the cunning contrivance of the
simony-engineers of our times. *O my soul come thou
not into their secrets.* As if they cared not to go to hell,
so be it were not the nearest way, but that they might
fetch a farre compasse round about. And yet father
Campian must not carry it so clearly, who taxeth the
Protestants for maintaining of simony. We confesse
it a personall vice amongst us, but not to be charged
as a Church-sinne, which by penall Laws it doth both
prohibit and punish. Did Rome herein look upon the
dust behind her own doores, she would have but little
cause to call her neighbour slut. What saith the Epi-
gram?

> *An Petrus fuerat Romæ sub judice lis est;*
> *Simonem Romæ nemo fuisse negat.*

> That Peter was at Rome, there's strife about it;
> That Simon was there, none did ever doubt it.

He hates corruption not onely in himself, but his servants. Otherwise it will do no good for the Master to throw bribes away, if the Men catch them up at the first rebound, yea before ever they come to the ground. Cambden can tell you what Lord-Keeper it was in the dayes of Queen Elizabeth, who though himself an upright man was hardly spoken of for the basenesse of his servants in the sale of Ecclesiasticall preferments.

When he hath freely bestowed a Living, he makes no boasts of it. To do this were a kind of spirituall simony, to ask and receive applause of others; as if the commonnesse of faulting herein made a right, and the rarity of giving things freely merited *ex condigno* a generall commendation. He expects nothing from the Clerk he presented but his prayers to God for him, respectfull carriage towards him, and painfulnesse in his Calling, who having gotten his place freely may discharge it the more faithfully: whereas those will scarce afford to feed their sheep fat, who rent the pasture at too high a rate.

To conclude, let Patrons imitate this particular example of King William Rufus, who (though sacrilegious in other acts) herein discharged a good conscience. Two Monks came to him to buy an Abbots place of him, seeking to outvie each other in offering great summes of money, whilest a third Monk stood by, and said nothing. To whom said the King, What wilt thou give for the place. Not a penny, answered he, for it is against my conscience; but here I stay to wait home on him whom your Royall pleasure shall designe Abbot. Then quoth the King, Thou of the three best deservest the place, and shalt have it, and so bestowed it on him.

CHAP. 13

The good Landlord

Is one that lets his land on a reasonable rate, so that the Tenant by employing his stock, and using his industry, may make an honest livelihood thereby, to maintain himself and his children.

His rent doth quicken his Tenant but not gall him. Indeed 'tis observed, that where Landlords are very easy, the Tenants (but this is *per Accidens*, out of their own lazinesse) seldome thrive, contenting themselves to make up the just measure of their rent, and not labouring for any surplusage of estate. But our Landlord puts some metall into his Tenants industry, yet not grating him too much, lest the Tenant revenge the Landlords cruelty to him upon his land.

Yet he raiseth his rents (or fines equivalent) in some proportion to the present price of other commodities. The plenty of money makes a seeming scarcity of all other things, and wares of all sorts do daily grow dear. If therefore our Landlord should let his rents stand still as his Grandfather left them, whilest other wares dayly go on in price, he must needs be cast farre behind in his estate.

What he sells or lets to his Tenant, he suffers him quietly to enjoy according to his covenants. This is a great joy to a Tenant, though he buyes dear to possesse without disturbance. A strange example there was of Gods punishing a covetous Landlord at Rye in Sussex, *Anno* 1570. He having a certain marish, wherein men on poles did dry their fishnets, received yearly of them a sufficient summe of money, till not content therewith he caused his servant to pluck up the poles, not suffering the fishermen to use them any longer, except they would compound at a greater rate. But it came to passe the same night that the sea breaking in covered the same marish with water, and so it still continueth.

He detests and abhorres all inclosure with depopulation. And because this may seem a matter of importance, we will break it into severall propositions.

1 *Inclosure may be made without depopulating.* Infinites of examples shew this to be true. But depopulation hath cast a slander on inclosure, which because often done with it, people suspect it cannot be done without it.

2 *Inclosure made without depopulating is injurious to none.* I mean if proportionable allotments be made to the poore for their commonage, and free & leaseholders have a considerable share with the lord of the mannour.

3 *Inclosure without depopulating is beneficiall to private persons.* Then have they most power and comfort to improve their own parts, and for the time, and manner thereof may mould it to their own conveniencie. The Monarch of one acre will make more profit thereof then he that hath his share in fourty in common.

4 *Inclosure without depopulating is profitable to the Commonwealth.* If injurious to no private person, and profitable to them all, it must needs be beneficiall to the Commonwealth, which is but the *Summa totalis* of sundry persons, as severall figures. Besides, if a Mathematician should count

the wood in the hedges, to what a mighty forrest would it amount? This underwood serves for supplies to save timber from burning, otherwise our wooden walls in the water must have been sent to the fire. Adde to this the strength of an inclosed Countrey against a forrein invasion. Hedges and counter-hedges (having in number what they want in height and depth) serve for barracadoes, and will stick as birdlime in the wings of the horse, and scotch the wheeling about of the foot. Small resistance will make the enemy to earn every mile of ground as he marches. Object not, That inclosure destroyes tillage, the staff of a countrey, for it need not all be converted to pasturage. Cain and Abel may very well agree in the Commonwealth, the Plowman and Shepherd part the inclosures betwixt them.

5 *Inclosure with depopulation is a canker to the Commonwealth.* It needs no proof: wofull experience shews how it unhouses thousands of people, till desperate need thrusts them on the gallows. Long since had this land been sick of a plurisie of people, if not let blood in their Western Plantations.

6 *Inclosure with depopulation endammageth the parties themselves.* 'Tis a paradox and yet a truth, that reason shews such inclosures to be gainfull, and experience proves them to be losse to the makers. It may be, because God being φιλάνθρωπος, a Lover of man, mankind, and mens society, and having said to them, *Multiply and increase*, counts it an affront unto him, that men depopulate, and whereas bees daily swarm, men make the hives

fewer. The margin shall direct you to the Authour that counts eleven mannours in Northhampton-shire thus inclosed: which towns have vomited out (to use his own expression) and unburthened themselves of their former desolating and de-populating owners, and I think of their posterity.

He rejoyceth to see his Tenants thrive. Yea he counts it a great honour to himself, when he perceiveth that God blesseth their endeavours, and that they come forward in the world. I close up all with this pleasant story. A Farmer rented a Grange generally reported to be haunted by Faries, and paid a shrewd rent for the same at each half years end. Now a Gentleman asked him how he durst be so hardy as to live in the house, and whether no Spirits did trouble him. *Truth* (said the Farmer) *there be two Saints in heaven vex me more then all the devils in hell, namely the Virgin Mary, and Michael the Archangel*; on which dayes he paid his rent.

Chap. 14

The good Master of a Colledge

The Jews *Anno* 1348. were banished out of most countreys of Christendome, principally for poysoning of springs and fountains. Grievous therefore is their offense, who infect Colledges, the fountains of learn-ing and religion; and it concerneth the Church and State, that the Heads of such houses be rightly quali-fied, such men as we come to character.

His learning if beneath eminency is farre above con-tempt. Sometimes ordinary scholars make extraordinary good Masters. Every one who can play well on Apollo's harp cannot skilfully drive his chariot, there being a peculiar mystery of Government. Yea as a little allay makes gold to work the better, so (perchance) some dulnesse in a man makes him fitter to manage secular affairs; and those who have climbed up Parnassus but half way better behold worldly businesse (as lying low and nearer to their sight) then such as have climbed up to the top of the mount.

He not onely keeps the Statutes (in his study) but observes them: for the maintaining of them will maintain him, if he be questioned. He gives them their true dimensions, not racking them for one, and shrinking them for another, but making his conscience his daily Visitour. He that breaks the Statutes, and thinks to rule better by his own discretion, makes many gaps in the hedge, and then stands to stop one of them with a stake in his hand. Besides, thus to confound the will of the dead Founders, is the ready way to make living mens charitie (like Sᵣ Hugh Willoughby in discovering the Northern passage) to be frozen to death, and will dishearten all future Benefactours.

He is principall Porter, and chief Chappell-monitour. For where the Master keeps his chamber alwayes, the scholars will keep theirs seldome, yea perchance may make all the walls of the Colledge to be gate. He seeks to avoid the inconvenience when the gates do rather divide then confine the scholars, when the Colledge is distinguished (as France into *Cis & Transalpina*) into the part on this, and on the otherside of the walls. As for out-lodgings (like galleries, necessary evils in populous Churches) he rather tolerates then approves them.

In his Elections he respecteth merit, not onely as the condition but as the cause thereof. Not like Leofricus Abbot of S. Albans, who would scarce admit any into his Convent though well deserving, except he was a Gentleman born. He more respects literature in a scholar, then great mens letters for him. A learned Master of a Colledge in Cambridge (since made a reverend Bishop, and, to the great grief of good men and great losse of Gods Church, lately deceased) refused a Mandate for choosing of a worthlesse man fellow. And when it was expected, that at the least he should have been outed of his Mastership for this his contempt, King James highly commended him, and encouraged him ever after to follow his own conscience, when the like occasion should be given him.

He winds up the Tenants to make good musick, but not to break them. Sure Colledge-lands were never given to fat the Tenants and sterve the scholars, but that both might comfortably subsist. Yea generally I heare the Muses commended for the best Land-ladies, and a Colledge-lease is accounted but as the worst kind of freehold.

He is observant to do all due right to Benefactours. If not piety, policy would dictate this unto him. And though he respects not Benefactours kinsmen, when at their first admission they count themselves born heirs apparent to all preferment which the house can heap on them, and therefore grow lazy & idle; yet he counts their alliance, seconded with mediocrity of desert, a strong title to Colledge-advancement.

He counts it lawfull to enrich himself, but in subordination to the Colledge good. Not like Varus, Governour of Syria, who came poore into the countrey, and found it rich, but departed thence rich, and left the countrey poore. Methinks 'tis an excellent commendation which Trinity Colledge in Cambridge in her records bestows on Doctour Still once Master thereof. *Se ferebat Patremfamilias providum, ἀγαθὸν κουρότροφον, nec Collegio gravis fuit aut onerosus.*

He disdains to nourish dissension amongst the members of his house. Let Machiavills Maxime, *Divide & regnabis*, if offering to enter into a Colledge-gate, sink thorow the grate, and fall down with the dirt. For besides that the fomenting of such discords agrees not with a good conscience, each party will watch advantages, and Pupils will often be made to suffer for their Tutours quarrells: *Studium partium* will be *magna pars studiorum*, and the Colledge have more rents then revenues.

He scorneth the plot, to make onely dunces Fellows, to the end he may himself command in chief. As thinking that they who know nothing, will do any thing, and so he shall be a figure amongst cyphers, a bee amongst drones. Yet oftentimes such Masters are justly met with, and they find by experience, that the dullest horses are not easiest to be reined. But our Master endeavours so to order his elections, that every Scholar may be fit to make a Fellow, and every Fellow a Master.

Chap. 15

The life of Dr Metcalf

Nicholas Metcalf Doctour of Divinity, extracted out of an ancient and numerous family of Gentry in Yorkshire, was Archdeacon of Rochester, & Chaplain to John Fisher the Bishop thereof; by whom this our Doctour was employed to issue forth the monies for the building of S. Johns Colledge in Cambridge. For Margaret Countesse of Richmond and Derby intending to graft S. Johns Colledge into the old stock of S. Johns Hospitall, referr'd all to the Bishop of Rochester, and he used Metcalf as an agent in all proceedings which did concern that Foundation: which will inferre him to be both a wise and an honest man.

Some make him to be but meanly learned; and one telleth us a long storie how a Sophister put a fallacie upon him, *à sensu diviso ad sensum compositum*, and yet the Doctours dimme eyes could not discern it. But such trifles were beneath him; and what wonder is it if a Generall long used in governing an armie, hath forgotten his school-play, and Fencers rules, to put by every thrust?

Doubtlesse, had not his learning been sufficient, Bishop Fisher, a great clerk himself, would not have placed him to govern the Colledge. But we know that some count all others but dry scholars, whose learning runneth in a different channell from their own: and it is possible, that the great distance betwixt men in matter of Religion might hinder the new learning in one to see the old learning in the other.

But grant that Metcalf, with Themistocles, could not fiddle, yet he could make a little city a great one: though dull in himself, he could whet others by his encouragement. He found the Colledge spending scarce two hundred marks by the yeare, he left it spending a thousand marks and more. For he not onely procured and settled many donations, and by-foundations (as we term them) of Fellowships, and

Scholarships, founded by other; but was a Benefactour himself, *Pro certis ornamentis & structuris in Capella, & pro ædificatione sex Camerarum à tergo Coquinæ*, &c. as it is evidenced in the Colledge books. He counted the Colledge his own home, and therefore cared not what cost he bestowed on it: not like those Masters, who making their Colledges as steps to higher advancement will trample on them to raise up themselves, and using their wings to flie up to their own honour, cannot afford to spread them to brood their Colledge. But the thriving of the nourcery, is the best argument to prove the skill and care of the nource. See what store of worthy men the house in his time did yield:

William Cecill, *Lord Burly*,
Sᵣ. John Cheek,   } *Statesmen.*
Walter Haddon.

Ralph Bain,   *Coventrie and Lichfield,*
John Christopherson,   *Chichester,*
Robert Horn,   *Bishop of*   *Winton,*
James Pilkinton,   *Duresme,*
John Tailour,   *Lincoln,*
Thomas Watson.   *Lincoln.*

Roger Ascham,
George Bullock,
Roger Hutchinson,   } *Learned writers.*
Alban Langdale,
John Seaton.

Hugh Fitz-Herbert,
William Jreland,
Laurence Pilkinton,   } *Learned Men.*
—— Tomson,
Henry Wright.

With very many more. For though I dare not say
that all these were old enough to bear fruit in Metcalfs
time, yet sure I am by him they were inoculated, and
in his dayes admitted into the Colledge.

Yet for all these his deserts Metcalf in his old age
was expell'd the Colledge, and driven out when he
could scarce go. A new generation grew up (advanced
by him) whose active spirits stumbled at his gravity
(young seamen do count ballast needlesse yea burthensome in a ship) and endeavoured his removall. It
appears not what particular fault they laid to his
charge. Some think that the Bishop of Rochester his
good lord being put to death, occasioned his ruine,
Fishers misfortune being Metcalfs highest misde-
meanour. He sunk with his Patron, and when his
sunne was set it was presently night with him: for
according to the Spanish proverb, *where goes the
bucket, there goes the rope,* where the principall mis-
carries, all the dependants fall with him.

Others conceive it was for his partiality in preferring Northern men, as if in his compasse there were
no points but such onely as looked to the North,
advancing alone his own countrey-men, and more
respecting their need then deserts. Indeed long before,
I find William Millington first Provost of Kings Colledge put out of his place, for his partiality in electing
Yorkshire men.

But herein Metcalf is sufficiently justified: for he
found Charity hottest in the cold countrey, *Northern
men were most partiall* (saith one) *in giving lands to the
Colledge, for the furtherance of learning.* Good reason
therefore Northern Scholars should be most watered
there, where Northern Benefactours rained most.

Well, good old Metcalf must forsake the House. Methinks the blushing bricks seem asham'd of their ingratitudes, and each doore, window, and casement in the Colledge, was a mouth to plead for him.

But what shall we say? Mark generally the grand deservers in States, and you shall find them lose their lustre before they end their life. The world, out of covetousnesse to save charges to pay them their wages, quarrelling with them, as if an over-merit were an offence. And whereas some impute this to the malignant influence of the heavens, I ascribe it rather to a pestilent vapour out of the earth; I mean, That rather men then starres are to be blamed for it.

He was twenty years Master, and on the 4 day of June 1537. went out of his office, and it seems dyed soon after: his Epitaph is fastned on a piece of brasse on the wall, in the Colledge-Chappell. We must not forget that all who were great doers in his expulsion, were great sufferers afterwards, and dyed all in great miserie. There is difference betwixt prying into Gods secrets, and being stark blind: Yea I question whether we are not bound to look where God points by so memorable a judgement, shewing that those branches most justly whithered which pluck'd up their own root.

CAMBRIDGE
PLAIN TEXTS

~⌒~

The following Volumes have recently
been added to this Series:

English

HENRYSON. The Testament of Cresseid.
With a Note by A. L. Attwater. 1s. 3d.

GOWER. Selections from Confessio Amantis.
With a Note by H. S. Bennett. 1s. 3d.

French

MOLIÈRE: La Critique de l'École des Femmes
and L'Impromptu de Versailles.
With a Note by A. Tilley. 1s. 3d.

German

HOFFMANN: Der Kampf der Sänger.
With a Note by G. Waterhouse. 1s. 6d.

LESSING: Hamburgische Dramaturgie I, II.
With a Note by G. Waterhouse. 1s. 6d. each

Spanish

OLD SPANISH BALLADS.
With a Note by J. P. Howard. 1s. 6d.

VILLENA, LEBRIJA, ENCINA. Selections
With a Note by I. Bullock. 1s. 6d.

small octavo pages of text, preceded
note on the author

LIMP CLOTH

German

GRILLPARZER. Der Arme Spielmann. Erinnerungen an
    Beethoven.
HERDER. Kleinere Aufsätze I.
HOFFMANN. Der Kampf der Sänger.
LESSING. Hamburgische Dramaturgie I.
LESSING. Hamburgische Dramaturgie II.

Italian

ALFIERI. La Virtù Sconosciuta.
GOZZI, GASPARO. La Gazzetta Veneta.
LEOPARDI. Pensieri.
MAZZINI. Fede e Avvenire.
ROSMINI. Cinque Piaghe.

Spanish

BOLIVAR, SIMON. Address to the Venezuelan Congress
    at Angostura, February 15, 1819.
CALDERÓN. La Cena de Baltasar.
CERVANTES. Prologues and Epilogue.
CERVANTES. Rinconete y Cortadillo.
ESPRONCEDA. El Estudiante de Salamanca.
LOPE DE VEGA. El Mejor Alcalde. El Rey.
LUIS DE LEON. Poesías Originales.
OLD SPANISH BALLADS.
VILLEGAS. El Abencerraje.
VILLENA: LEBRIJA: ENCINA. Selections.

SOME PRESS OPINIONS

"These are delightful, slim little books....The print is very clear and pleasant to the eye....These Cambridge Plain Texts are just the kind of book that a lover of letters longs to put in his pocket as a prophylactic against boredom." THE NEW STATESMAN

"These little books....are exquisitely printed on excellent paper and are prefaced in each case by a brief biographical note concerning the author: otherwise entirely unencumbered with notes or explanatory matter, they form the most delicious and companionable little volumes we remember to have seen. The title-page is a model of refined taste—*simplex munditiis*." THE ANGLO-FRENCH REVIEW

"With their admirable print, the little books do credit to the great Press which is responsible for them." NOTES AND QUERIES

"The series of texts of notable Italian works which is being issued at Cambridge should be made known wherever there is a chance of studying the language; they are clear, in a handy form, and carefully edited....The venture deserves well of all who aim at the higher culture." THE INQUIRER

"Selections of this kind, made by competent hands, may serve to make us acquainted with much that we should otherwise miss. To read two of Donne's tremendous sermons may send many readers eagerly to enlarge their knowledge of one of the great glories of the English pulpit." THE HOLBORN REVIEW

"This new Spanish text-book, printed on excellent paper, in delightfully clear type and of convenient pocket size, preserves the high level of achievement that characterises the series." THE TEACHER'S WORLD *on* "Cervantes: Prologues and Epilogue"

"It is difficult to praise too highly the Cambridge Plain Texts." THE LONDON MERCURY

www.ingramcontent.com/pod-product-compliance
Ingram Content Group UK Ltd.
Pitfield, Milton Keynes, MK11 3LW, UK
UKHW042148280225
455719UK00001B/187

9 781107 697362